God is the Best Artist!

THE STORY OF ZACHARIAH'S ACRES

God Is the Best Artist!
The Story of Zachariah's Acres

Zachariah's Acres, Inc. © 2021

All rights reserved. Use of any part of this publication, whether reproduced, transmitted in any form or by any means, electronic, mechanical, photocopying, recording, or otherwise, or stored in a retrieval system, without the prior consent of Zachariah's Acres, Inc., except by reviewers and media, who may quote brief passages in a review or an article giving credit to Zachariah's Acres, Inc., is an infringement of copyright law and is forbidden.

Please feel free to share the message of Zachariah's Acres, as it is the purpose of this publication.

While Zachariah's Acres, Inc. and the production team have used their best efforts in preparing this book, they make no representations or warranties with respect to the accuracy or completeness of this book and specifically disclaim any implied warranties of merchantability or fitness for a particular purpose. Neither Zachariah's Acres, Inc. nor the production team shall be liable for any loss of profit or any other commercial damages, including but not limited to special, incidental, consequential, or other damages from advice or ideas received from this book.

The publisher and author shall have neither liability nor responsibility to any person or entity with respect to loss, damage, or injury caused or alleged to be caused directly or indirectly by the information contained in this book.

Bible references from New International Version (NIV) unless otherwise specified. Verses without citations paraphrased.

Conceived by God
Photography by AB Designs, Caleb Enockson Photography, Rachael Carlson, and the Servants of Zachariah's Acres
Written by Emily Enockson
Edited by Megan Terry
Cover Design by Rachael Carlson
Interior Design by Fusion Creative Works
Book Production by Aloha Publishing
Executive Producer: Alan Petelinsek
Editor-in-Chief: Terry Bartowitz

Print ISBN: 978-1-7360577-0-4

For more information, visit ZachariahsAcres.org

Printed in Canada

This book is dedicated to children with special needs and their families.

May God be glorified in all His designs!

"Truly I tell you, if you have faith as small as a mustard seed, you can say to this mountain, 'Move from here to there,' and it will move. Nothing will be impossible for you."

—Matthew 17:20

Table of Contents

Who We Are 9
    FACES of ZA: Noah and Maya 18

Our Story, God's Glory 19
    Who Is Zachariah? 20
    Schmeckpeper Family 32
    Luke 34

Our Vision and Values 35
    Kathryn 44
    Maya 46
    Power Test, Inc 51
    Josie 52

Our Community 53
    Our Volunteers - Testimonials 60
    Spring Creek Church 61
    Community Partners 64
    David 66
    Molly 70
    Angelique 72

Lessons From Our Community 79
    Truths From Our Campus 87

Get Involved 101

Our mission is to connect children with special needs, and their families, to the miracles of nature so they may know their Creator.

Who We Are

Zachariah's Acres (ZA) is a one-of-a-kind place where children with special needs find purpose and belonging and explore God's Creation. When guests visit our universally designed campus, nature, wildlife, and agricultural experiences are accessible to all. Our focus is serving the underserved—individuals of all ages with cognitive and physical disabilities are welcomed with open arms. Zachariah's Acres is a beautiful setting where families challenged by special healthcare needs feel acknowledged and loved as they experience new adventures together.

THE STORY OF ZACHARIAH'S ACRES

The Campus

Zachariah's Acres is a nonprofit 501(c)(3) located in the town of Oconomowoc, Wisconsin. We are uniquely positioned on 48 glorious acres surrounded by nature, serenity, and amazing landscape.

Our campus features an ADA-compliant fishing pier, stocked fishing pond, walking and rolling paths, raised gardens, greenhouses, garden workshop, accessible tree house with a wildlife observation deck, heated barn, patio, and bonfire gathering area. Volunteers and guests have enriched the landscape with thousands of evergreen trees, raised garden beds, a fruit orchard, and acres of wildflowers and prairie grasses. The campus allows families and guests to recharge for a few hours or an afternoon and connect with their Creator by immersing themselves in nature.

The Need

Imagine never experiencing nature up close. Consider never having an opportunity to be in a garden, a forest, or the middle of a field, or being unable to pick strawberries because you can't reach them, aren't welcome, or it may not be safe for you. No roasting marshmallows, no searching for caterpillars, no picking fruit or flowers, no snowball fights, no playing in leaves, no fireflies. This is the reality for many kids with disabilities. Because nature isn't always accessible, they can't have these experiences. They can at Zachariah's Acres.

Out of almost 900,000 children in Wisconsin public schools, 14 percent have a disability—cognitive, physical, or a combination. This equates to 126,000 potential annual guests for Zachariah's Acres and doesn't capture anybody under the age of 5 or over the age of 21.

We serve a precious part of our population that is often ignored. Great change starts with the acknowledgment that these special individuals exist in our world and they have an eternal purpose.

"My grace is sufficient for you, for my power is made perfect in weakness."

—2 Corinthians 12:9

At ZA, children of all ages with special needs can use their gifts for God's glory. We're intentional about nature-based activities that allow our guests to shine and experience something that they would never get a chance to do elsewhere.

We believe all lives have value. God has gifted each of us. While our guests don't lead "normal" lives, they were created on purpose, for a purpose.

Disabilities touch all nationalities and demographics. Someone does not have to be born with a special need to acquire one. A permanent physical and/or cognitive challenge does not diminish the eternal beauty of one's life.

Nature is an equalizer, something everyone can appreciate. It should be accessible to everyone.

How We Serve

The vision for Zachariah's Acres grew from one question, many voices, and one collective idea: outdoor activities provide life experiences that cannot be replicated or replaced. We are committed to enhancing the landscape and making it accessible for children with special needs and their families to have meaningful experiences in nature.

We provide the following:

- A setting where children with disabilities are comfortable in the outdoors and participate in fully accessible agricultural and nature-based activities

- A place where families, organizations, and community members gather to play, share fellowship, relax, and learn

- Events and programs that allow families and children to enjoy enriching experiences and new adventures to enhance and enrich their lives

- A neutral setting where special needs children and young adults learn social and vocational skills through responsibility, enthusiasm, teamwork, positive attitudes, and work ethic

ZACHARIAH'S ACRES

478 Dedicated Volunteers

Nature-based experiences exclusively for children with special needs and their families

37,000+
GUESTS SERVED SINCE 2012

86 COMMUNITY PARTNERS

NONPROFITS
BUSINESSES
CHURCHES
SCHOOLS

48 ACRES IN THE TOWN OF OCONOMOWOC, WISCONSIN

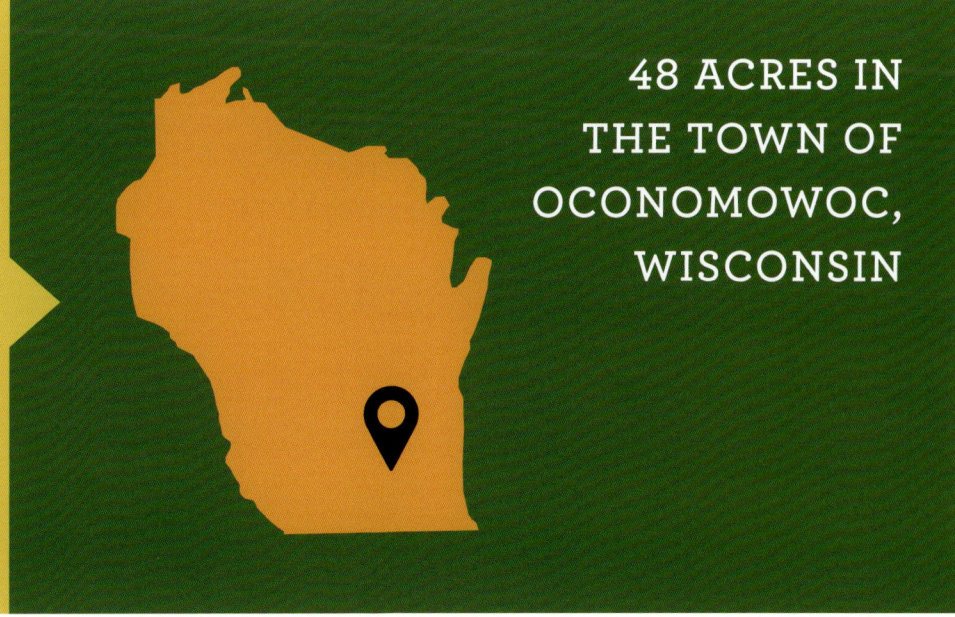

THE STORY OF ZACHARIAH'S ACRES

The FACES of ZA

"Zachariah's Acres is a safe space that doesn't just 'make room' for my son, but was conceived specifically for kids like him. It may seem like a small distinction but the difference between being welcome somewhere and just being able to be somewhere is tremendous for those of us always struggling to find a safe space in the world."

—The Haldorson Family

"We have been so happy to be able to participate in what ZA has had to offer. I can't even put into words the feelings that wash over me when we pull into the parking lot there. It is a community of acceptance and belonging and a chance for me to unite Maya with God's Creation."

—Holly and Maya Owens

Our Story, God's Glory

"For it is by grace you have been saved, through faith—and this is not from yourselves, it is the gift of God—not by works, so that no one can boast."

—Ephesians 2:8-9

Who Is Zachariah?

Zachariah is a boy who wants to be accepted and loved. He appreciates the outdoors and enjoys God's Creation. Zachariah is the son of Terry (ZA's volunteer President) and his wife, Tammy.

Our youngest was born early, but healthy. He was thriving in the NICU, so we left to spend time with our recently adopted children. The phone rang around 3:30 a.m. A stranger alerted us that our son "coded," and we needed to return to the hospital immediately. Upon arriving, there were numerous healthcare professionals surrounding his bed. A neonatologist asked our permission to unplug Zachariah as he had suffered a major heart attack, a significant stroke, died, been resuscitated, and was not expected to survive the next hour. While many devastating diagnoses were ascribed to our son, we determined not to agree with the prescribed outcomes.

While he has not taken an independent step nor spoken a word, Zachariah (which literally translates to "remembrance of the Lord") has touched many lives and brought some to know Jesus. Zachariah is an absolute gift packaged in a special way, and we are blessed beyond measure. God has always been faithful to us, and we will continue to be faithful to Him. He made a way where there was no way.

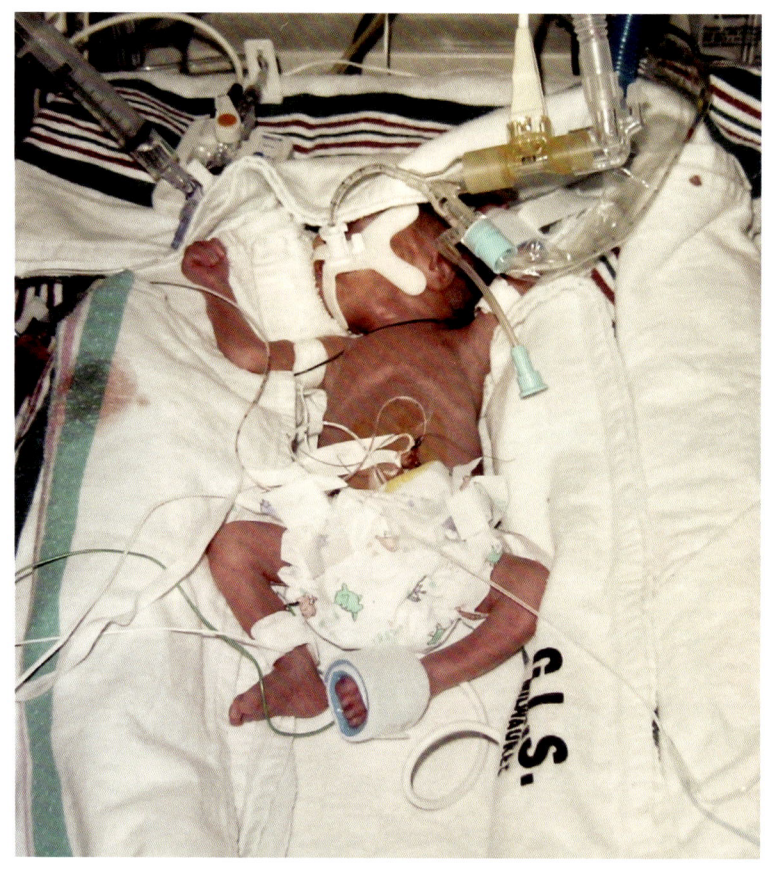

> "We praise God for His Son; we praise God for our son!"
>
> —Parents of Zachariah

Our Father, who art in heaven; hallowed by Thy name.

Thy kingdom come, Thy will be done, on earth as it is in heaven.

Give us this day our daily bread.

And forgive us our trespasses, as we forgive those who trespass against us.

And lead us not into temptation, but deliver us from evil.

For Thine is the Kingdom, and the power, and the glory, forever and ever.

Amen.

—The Lord's Prayer

GOD IS THE BEST ARTIST!

Land Acquisition

A mutual friend prodded two strangers to meet for coffee in March 2010. Both gentlemen were blessed, faithful servants who were determined to serve those frequently overlooked by our fast-paced society.

Due diligence, personal experience, community meetings, one-on-one interviews, and focus groups yielded the resounding need to acknowledge, accommodate, and love children with special healthcare needs and their families.

In October 2011, banquet tents were erected on a farm field in Oconomowoc, Wisconsin. Through basic promotion, and because of an unmet need, 224 guests enjoyed hay wagon rides, pumpkin bowling, and a pheasant and quail release. Fun, nature-based experiences resulted in a memorable day for all—children with special needs, siblings, parents, and volunteers.

After an enormous amount of praying and planning, acreage was acquired, then Zachariah's Acres was born. The mission was revealed by God, our Chairman of the Board: Connect children with special needs, and their families, to the miracles of nature so they may know their Creator. With growing faith and intentional work, tens of thousands of special guests have enjoyed God's artistry in nature and realized they are part of His plan.

Humble Beginnings

We hosted our first Fall Harvest Fest in an alfalfa field, the future home of the ZA campus. Volunteers worked all week to construct a tent for shelter, lay portable milking mats to make the land accessible, and devise engaging activities for the guests. Simple nature-based activities such as hay wagon rides, pumpkin bowling, and a hike/roll brought families together and formed the basis of our programming.

GOD IS THE BEST ARTIST!

First accessible garden beds built by Eagle Scout candidates and cared for by our guests

THE STORY OF ZACHARIAH'S ACRES

GOD IS THE BEST ARTIST!

Accessibility in the winter in Wisconsin proved to be a challenge, so we would close from November through May. The first three years we served 1,300 people under banquet tents in a farm field. A local bus company helped transport families to our event location while volunteers donated time to set up and tear down.

After the bus with a chair lift got stuck in the mud, a guest with his walker traveled the length of three city blocks through difficult terrain to get to our tent site. This young man's walker was so caked with mud the wheels weren't turning anymore. But when we asked if we could help him, he said, "*No, I want to finish this.*" His can-do attitude continues to inspire us to serve families year-round, regardless of weather.

> We serve excuseless, heroic people.

THE STORY OF ZACHARIAH'S ACRES

2012

- Land rezoned
- Nonprofit status achieved

2013

- Accessible fishing pier
- Stocked pond
- Land acquired

2014

- Multi-purpose barn
- 3/4 acre fruit orchard

2015

- Honey bees and chickens
- Increased accessibility via paving

2016

- Paved patio with firepit
- Garden Basket CSA
- Boardwalk to Prayer House

GOD IS THE BEST ARTIST!

The Zachariah's Acres Campus

The county mandated that we install a public road with a cul-de-sac. An asphalt road and driveway were paved and named Servants' Way, a reminder for our team and guests that they are not only selfless servants, but also the hands and feet of Jesus.

In 2014, the first permanent structure was constructed on the Zachariah's Acres campus. "The Barn" is a multi-purpose, heated gathering space that allows us to serve year-round, regardless of weather.

Our campus has expanded to include an accessible tree house, two chicken coops, garden workshop, accessible fishing pier, prayer house, firepit and gathering area, greenhouses, fruit orchard, thousands of trees, and acres of prairie grass and wildflowers.

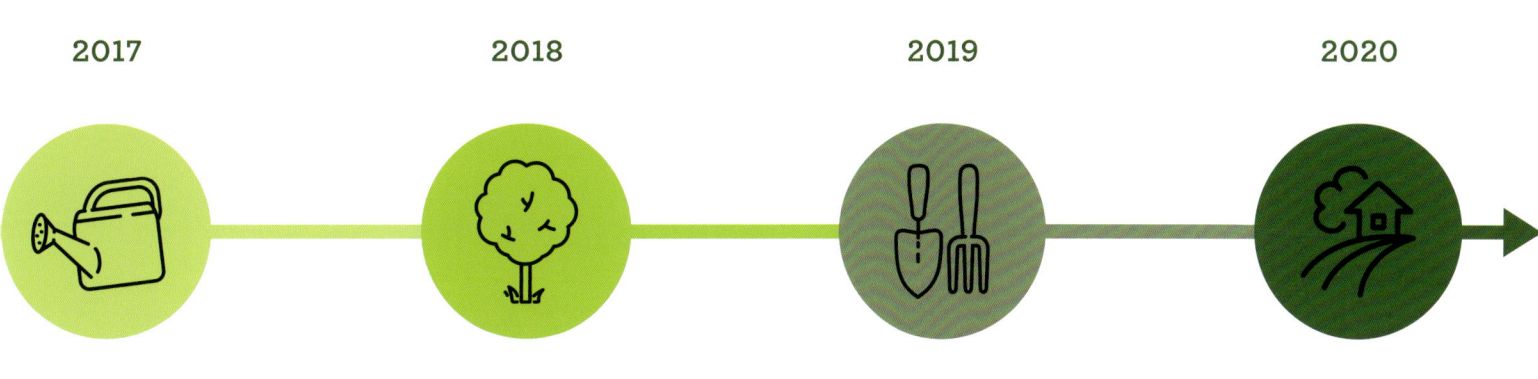

2017
- Year-round greenhouse
- 10,000-square-foot butterfly garden
- Accessible raised garden beds

2018
- Accessible tree house
- Maya's Music Terrace
- Additional 1,200 square feet of accessible garden beds

2019
- Garden workshop (second year-round building)

2020
- Production greenhouse
- Additional parking lot

THE STORY OF ZACHARIAH'S ACRES

The Co-Authors of ZA

Our guests are the co-authors of Zachariah's Acres, helping us continually improve through collaboration. Through servitude, it was incrementally unveiled who our service model was to exemplify: the greatest servant leader, Jesus.

During all of the challenges in obtaining zoning, community involvement, and fundraising, we prioritized the needs of our guests by simply serving. Volunteers and the ZA team developed nature-based experiences made just for special children, learning and growing together.

We found it abundantly important to consistently express to our guests, "You are the author of your life. You can do great things because you are made in His image."

Our service model encourages guests to gain self-confidence, which enables them to be more productive in their households, in their schools, and in their community. In some cases, they may even pursue a job they wouldn't have had the confidence to apply for before they came to Zachariah's Acres. We want to make an eternal difference in the lives of our guests, so we provide them with experiences that help them grow and live a life of meaning and purpose.

THE STORY OF ZACHARIAH'S ACRES

The FACES of ZA

The Schmeckpeper family loves spending time together outside, exploring all seasons, and learning new things. Dante, Mae, Rachel, and Jason started attending Zachariah's Acres in 2014. They immediately felt acknowledged and accepted by volunteers. Rachel shared she feels ZA is *"a welcoming place where we don't have to worry and can just be a family. We can just be ourselves."*

Dante and Mae get excited when they see a ZA event on the family calendar and wonder what fun and exciting activities the volunteers have dreamed up. Their favorite seasonal activities include roasting s'mores around the bonfire, snowshoeing, apple picking, collecting eggs from the coops, and sending a fish down the "Perch Plunge."

> **"**Snowshoeing is my favorite, and we get to find special things in the woods like deer antlers.**"**
>
> —Dante

GOD IS THE BEST ARTIST!

"Zachariah's Acres feels like home. We are treated with respect, understanding, love, and care. The beauty of nature surrounds you like your favorite comforter. We feel renewed, recharged, and at peace every time we come. Our family feels so blessed for all the wonderful memories that will last a lifetime. Thank you!"

—Jenny Lalko (parent)

"My students bloom at Zachariah's Acres! Just when we think we have had the best experience, we go back and it tops our last one!"

—Gerilyn (special educator)

Luke

Luke and Kathy Biernat have been part of the Zachariah's Acres community since 2013. Luke loves to go for UTV rides, fish at Shepherd's Pond, and make a s'more at the bonfire pit. The first time they attended, Luke made a craft, ate lots of snacks, and when it was time to leave, he didn't want to go. Volunteers were holding a prayer service after the event and Luke's family ended their first experience at ZA singing, praying, and thanking God for a beautiful day. Several years later, Luke had turned 18 and Kathy asked if they would still be allowed to return. We answered, *"As one of God's children, he is welcome."* Kathy and Luke are regular participants at family events, but Kathy has also invited her students from St. Mary's Parish to volunteer at ZA on a monthly basis.

"I wanted my family to experience God's beauty in the trees, lakes, gardens, and animals, but most importantly in the people who truly live as Jesus. My favorite line from a Church song is, 'Help me to see you in all I serve.' This is what ZA means to me. Each person you meet treats every guest and family member with love and sees Jesus in every face. While he may not be able to tell us in words, he tells us in his actions—Luke knows here he is loved and valued, and there are always s'mores."

—Kathy Biernat

Our Vision and Values

"Let the little children come to me, and do not hinder them, for the Kingdom of God belongs to such as these. Truly I tell you, anyone who will not receive the Kingdom of God like a little child will never enter it."

—Mark 10:14-15

Our Vision

Our vision focuses on children with special needs and their families:

To acknowledge, ease, and enrich their lives.

To make previously inaccessible nature-based activities accessible to them.

To proclaim the worth and beauty of each and every human being.

To let them know that God created all people and all things on purpose for a purpose.

To let them know that God loves them and desires to spend eternity with them.

> "'Love the Lord your God with all your heart and with all your soul and with all your mind.' This is the first and greatest commandment. And the second is like it: 'Love your neighbor as yourself.'"
>
> —Matthew 22:37-39

F.A.C.E.S.

The core values of Zachariah's Acres are faith, authenticity, compassion, excellence, and servitude (FACES).

Staff and volunteers live out each value when making decisions, interacting with guests, developing partnerships, preparing for events, and communicating in all forms.

We want our guests to understand that they are inherently valuable and that they are capable of more than they know. We acknowledge and love our special guests and encourage them to achieve more than they may have believed possible. We live our values by serving selflessly.

  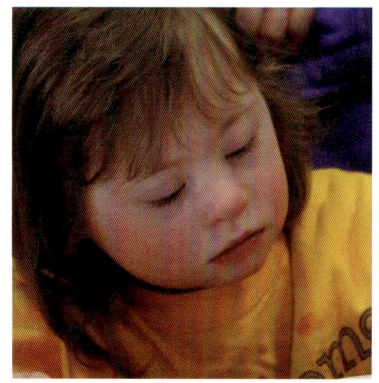 

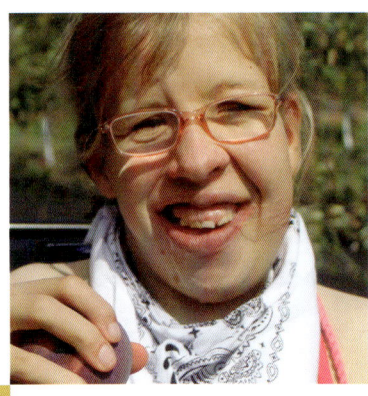  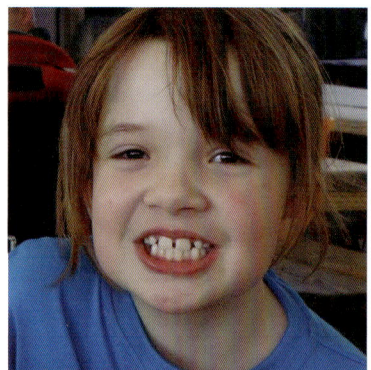 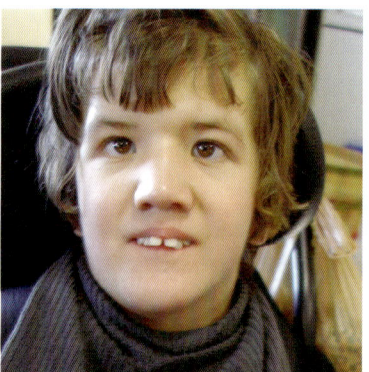

GOD IS THE BEST ARTIST!

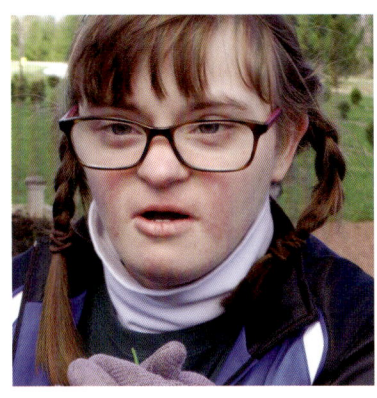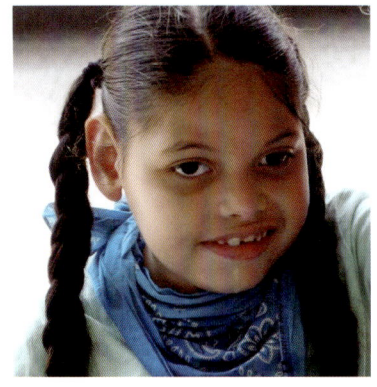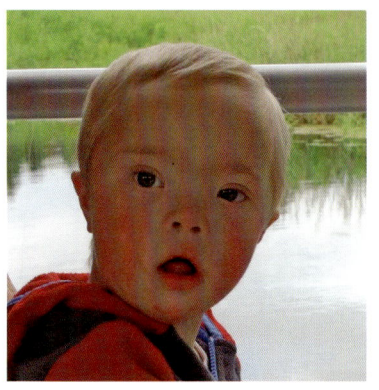
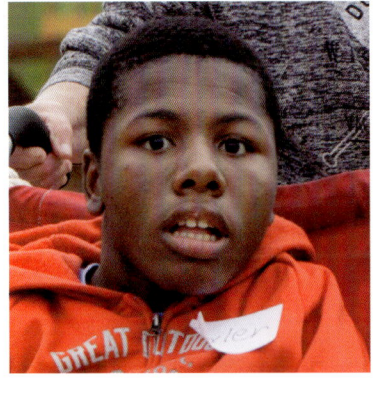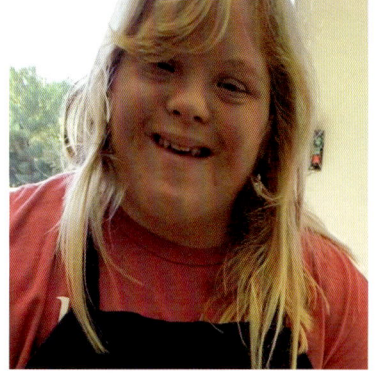
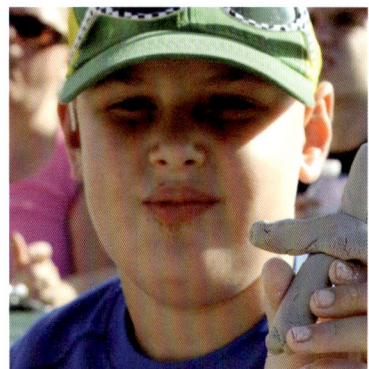

THE STORY OF ZACHARIAH'S ACRES

Faith

By going outside, you connect with God's Creation. Regardless of your ability or disability, you can experience wonder and awe. In that way, nature is an equalizer. When you hear leaves blowing in the wind or see a wildflower, it gives you pause to contemplate and say, "Nature was created by someone greater than I. As a human, I can't replicate that."

Faith is the foundation of our ministry and is strengthened for volunteers, guests, and families on a daily basis. Children with special needs have a unique ability to make you appreciate the small things in life, to stop and observe nature in a way you never have before. It's remarkable to watch a kid's face light up when he picks a carrot from the dirt rather than the refrigerated section at the grocery store.

What you do speaks so loudly that what you say I cannot hear.

"He said to them, 'Let the little children come to me, and do not hinder them, for the kingdom of God belongs to such as these. Truly I tell you, anyone who will not receive the kingdom of God like a little child will never enter it.'"

—Mark 10:14-15

Mark 10:14-15 is one of many scriptures posted at Zachariah's Acres. The Bible verses are reminders of Whom we serve by acknowledging, accepting, and loving children with special needs. We were pleasantly surprised when one of our guests looked up from his wheelchair and asked, *"Who is that Mark guy?"* This inquiry came from a grade school student from the largest school district in our state. Fifteen minutes later, he and his teacher were still discussing the Gospel! This special little boy may use a wheelchair, but he was reaching for Heaven with child-like simplicity and receptivity.

Authenticity

Authenticity means raising the bar of expectation for our guests and loving them unconditionally. Our guests are authentic, honest, and real with us, so they should expect authenticity from us as well.

Our guests are brilliant, but people often don't have enough patience to let them show, in their own way, their skill sets. Children with special needs develop a sixth sense for authenticity. They know right away whether you're sincerely interested or just another adult who underestimates them. They can sense it through your actions, how you approach them, and your facial expression. Do you recall their name? Do you make eye contact? We stretch our guests because we know they're capable of so much.

By using our two ears and one mouth proportionately, we help our special guests learn hope, love, comfort, trust, and confidence.

"A new command I give you: Love one another. As I have loved you, so you must love one another. By this everyone will know that you are my disciples, if you love one another."

—John 13:34-35

"Therefore, my dear brothers and sisters, stand firm. Let nothing move you. Always give yourselves fully to the work of the Lord, because you know that your labor in the Lord is not in vain."

—1 Corinthians 15:58

Kathryn

Kathryn visits Zachariah's Acres with her friends from the YMCA on weekdays and also attends weekend activities at ZA with her family. Kathryn has a lively personality and can be very determined to get her own way. On one of her visits, we invited Kathryn to go snowshoeing, but she refused to because of the cold. With a little patience and gentle encouragement from ZA volunteers, we learned Kathryn was hesitant because she didn't think she could do it and was scared. The whole team cheered her on as she put aside her fears to try something new. Her mom shared later that day, *"You changed my daughter's life. Going snowshoeing helped build her confidence and that has translated to other places in her life."*

Compassion

Real compassion is acknowledging someone for who they are and serving them with dignity.

We treat our special guests like royalty because they are God's children. We acknowledge them the moment they arrive on our campus, opening doors; smiling; using first names to greet them; and offering a high five, fist bump, or positive display of joy and acknowledgment.

We choose to see our guests as God does, miracles made in His image. We treat each individual with kindness, look them in the eye, ask age-appropriate questions, and show unconditional love.

The guests we serve are excuseless, silent sufferers. Their life experiences include therapies, surgeries, medications, separation, isolation, and utter desperation.

Compassion is placing your needs aside to care for others who are hurting. It is allowing your heart to bleed for them and be moved to act on their behalf.

"Therefore, as God's chosen people, holy and dearly loved, clothe yourselves with compassion, kindness, humility, gentleness, and patience."

—Colossians 3:12

Maya

Maya and Holly Owens began attending Zachariah's Acres in 2011. Holly was looking for a way to provide her daughter fun, new outdoor experiences and to feed her love of nature. It wasn't a simple task, as Maya's medical needs and physical limitations restricted the places they could visit.

The first time Holly and Maya visited ZA, it was an alfalfa field. But Maya's love for adventure propelled them to get outside and explore. Upon arrival Maya exclaimed, *"Mama! This is so beautiful. Look at the trees and the clouds!"* She saw the beauty in the natural landscape, not just a dirt road and farm field. Maya and Holly became regulars at ZA family events, watching the campus transform from a dirt road and tents to paved paths and an accessible barn with changing tables, heat, and running water.

From spring afternoons flying kites and taking hayrides to summer evenings picking strawberries and feeding chickens, the new experiences blended with the steadfast seasonal ones. Maya enjoyed pumpkin bowling in the fall, hayrides with new friends, and later

on visiting with "buddies." ZA events provided a much needed respite for Holly not in task, but in conversation. Sleigh rides and Santa graced their winter visits while flower-picking and handcrafted gifts captured Mother's Day memories.

Zachariah's Acres became a sanctuary for Maya and Holly, a place Maya could be herself—the girl who loved nature, not the girl with all the medical issues. It opened Holly's eyes to God's perfect plan.

Excellence

The word excellence tends to make people think about an unattainable level of skill or achievement, but it's about holding yourself accountable to God's commandments.

We hold each other accountable to our values and work as a team. Board members volunteer at event registration, load Christmas trees on cars, and plant in the garden. We are dedicated teammates working together, serving through action.

Excellence is about carrying out our work to the best of our ability and serving others selflessly. We work toward a shared vision and remain accountable to our Creator, who is the Chairman of our Board.

Our staff and volunteers approach projects with a fresh perspective, positive attitude, and strong work ethic. We stay flexible, continually improving and learning.

After every fundraising event, school group, or family experience, we ask ourselves, "How can we do this a little bit better, a little bit different?" Most people are okay with good enough, but we're constantly finding ways to improve. It's challenging, but it's also fulfilling.

> "From everyone who has been given much, much will be demanded; and from the one who has been entrusted with much, much more will be asked."
>
> —Luke 12:48

Excellence in Action

Accessibility is a key component of serving children with special needs. In the early spring of 2015 we hosted an event on a muddy April day. The bonfire pit was loosely constructed of elevated bricks surrounded by milking mats. That day, as the frost covered the ground, the mats became inaccessible and unusable. Something needed to change. John Craig of Century Landscaping donated time and materials to create a beautiful patio and bonfire gathering area for our guests. It was constructed just in time for our next event. This area is one of the most popular stations at Zachariah's Acres.

THE STORY OF ZACHARIAH'S ACRES

Servitude

Our ministry is built upon a foundation of servitude—heartfelt, intentional action to help others. Servitude requires being present and observing your surroundings to find what needs to be done and taking action. True servitude also means having a positive attitude. To serve, you must shift from your needs to the needs of others.

People throughout our community volunteer at Zachariah's Acres. These volunteers often sense the power of eternal impact by serving those who cannot pay them back.

It's powerful to witness people who come to give and serve yet leave with energy derived from fulfillment.

"I enjoy watching the faces of our guests and seeing God's joy in them while we accomplish common goals. Helping children and families experience all the activities that we offer makes all of our hard work worth it!"
—Garrett Bartowitz (Director of Buildings and Grounds)

"Whatever you do, work at it with all your heart, as working for the Lord, not for human masters."

—Colossians 3:23

Power Test, Inc.

Alan Petelinsek and Power Test, Inc. have supported ZA and our special guests since our inception via volunteering, attending fundraisers, construction, and service days. The team from Power Test, Inc. has increased accessibility to our campus through wooden benches, hay wagon ramps, and raised garden beds.

> "It is always easy to find help for my building projects at ZA. Everyone knows it is a great place with great people doing great things!"
>
> —Gregg Johnson (production manager)

Josie

Josie is a young lady who loves being outside, sunshine, and hanging out with her friends. Josie also happens to have CP and autism and is non-verbal. She attended the first event in 2011 with her family and had a very tough day. Nobody stared at them or asked them to leave, but instead offered to help get food or find a quiet place to relax. ZA is one of Josie's favorite places to visit. She especially loves going for golf cart rides, enjoying a salad with lettuce grown from the gardens, hanging out in the tree house with friends, or riding the hay wagon around the campus.

> "I see Jesus through the people at Zachariah's Acres."
>
> —Josie Enockson

Our Community

"A generous person will prosper; whoever refreshes others will be refreshed."

—Proverbs 11:25

Community of Zachariah's Acres

Tens of thousands of guests have been served through the generous support of the community, board members, businesses, churches, high schools, universities, foundations, and individuals. Our ministry expands and grows in direct relation to community involvement.

Volunteers show their support through serving on a regular basis at family events, company workdays, and church service days, as well as working alongside guests.

A group of parochial students volunteered to help our special guests plant seeds, clear brush, and prepare for an upcoming event. The students were gently nudged outside of their comfort zones by acknowledging peers who have special needs. One student declared, *"I learned to put my faith into action today at ZA."*

St. Mary's Visitation School

> "Called by Christ to serve others, St. Mary's Visitation School, Elm Grove, sends students to ZA to make its Gospel teaching alive and present in this world. Working side by side with the guests of this amazing little slice of heaven, students see firsthand the inherent dignity and blessing each person brings to this life. Together they laugh, bond, plan, work, and play on the many acres of ZA, each moment renewing their understanding that each of us is created in God's image—and 'It is good,' so good!"

—Gary Newman
(SMV Jr. High theology teacher)

Thank You, Community Partners

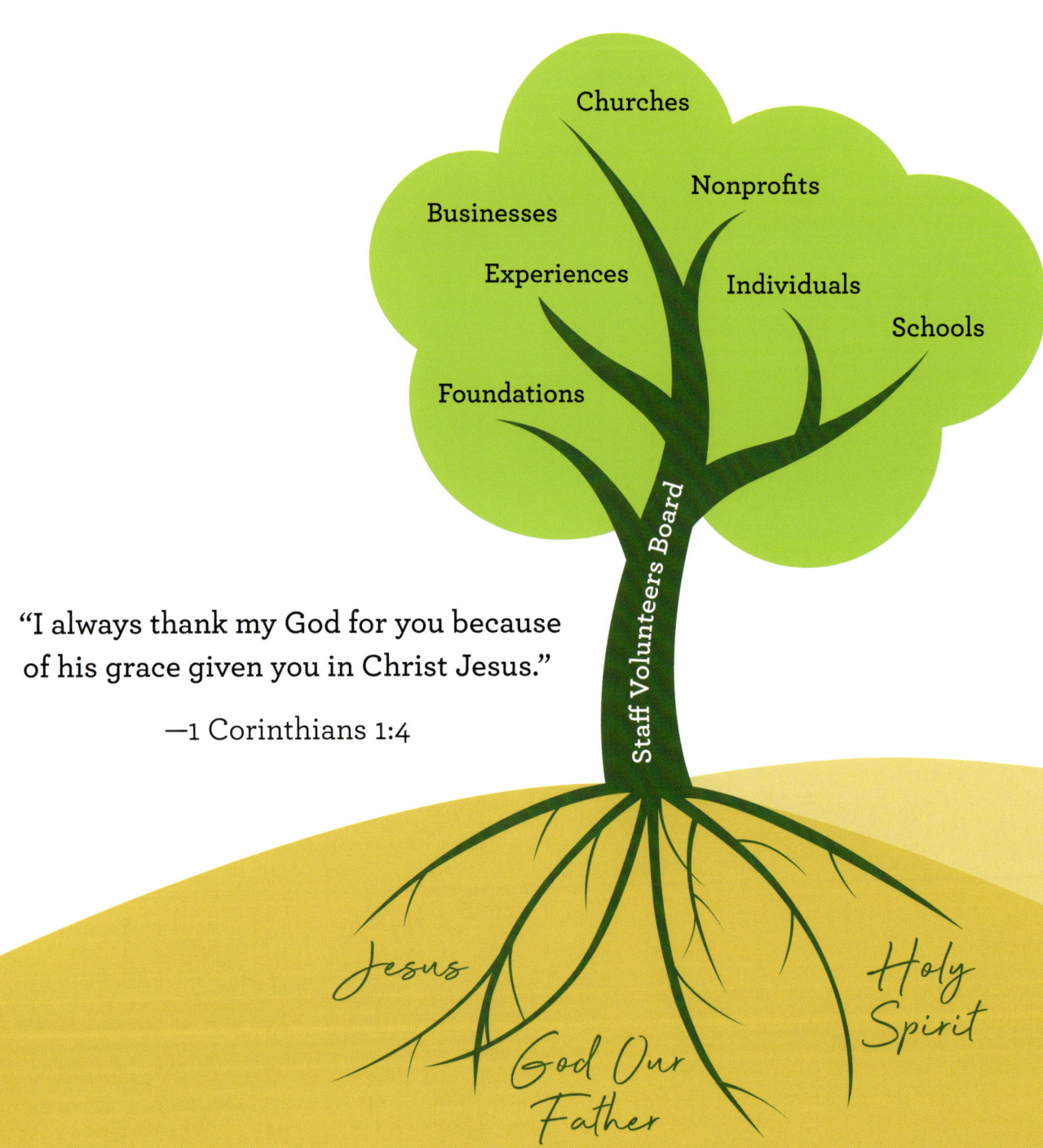

"I always thank my God for you because of his grace given you in Christ Jesus."

—1 Corinthians 1:4

Our Special Guests

When parents and guests share their experiences at ZA, overwhelming themes of joy, acknowledgment, adventure, hope, comfort, and contentment arise. One parent shared, *"Zachariah's Acres is a place where all of God's children can experience the beauty of nature and His love shining through every volunteer."* The support of our community allows guests to discover true hope, joy, and love in God's amazing Creation.

"My favorite things about Zachariah's Acres are feeding the chickens, fishing at the pond, and picking and eating strawberries and blueberries."

—Charlie (guest)

"I'm thankful for a safe place without worries."

—Kevin (guest)

"Zachariah's Acres is awesome, amazing, and great!"

—Andy (guest)

"At ZA I'm able to be myself, without judgment."

—Trenten (guest)

THE STORY OF ZACHARIAH'S ACRES

Our Families

One of the most beautiful and unexpected blessings of Zachariah's Acres is the rich community between parents, caregivers, volunteers, and siblings. Relationships and social skills are often difficult to foster for families with loved ones who have special needs. Families have come to rely on our events as a time to connect with others who understand what it is like to live in an atypical world.

"When I think about Zachariah's Acres, I'm thankful for so much: the wonderful volunteers who help all the families, the people who donate so that families like mine can have a safe place to explore nature and be in God's presence, and the amazing projects that they come up with for people to do. Because of Zachariah's Acres and the volunteers, my son can fish with people who know what they're doing, because I don't have a clue."

—Juanita (parent)

"As a mother of a child with special needs, I am thankful for the fun and interesting things that motivate my son to stand and walk on his own until he is completely exhausted. I'm also thankful to be able to relax and let go, even for just a few minutes."

—Barb (parent)

A Place of Hope and Connection

"Our family attended the very first event at Zachariah's Acres, back when you parked your car and trekked over the acreage to large white tents. Right away we sensed we were cared about. We found a place that was safe for all of us to be. There were many sensory activities for our daughter to explore, including a hay wagon ride where, when our daughter decided to lay on the floor to feel the vibrations as the tractor moved, no one judged her. At Zachariah's Acres, we can chat with other families or new friends around the firepit or recharge in the tree house. The frequent question in all of our minds is 'Why?' Why are we given such an incredible place to rest and renew, graced by volunteers who bless us through supporting and caring for all of the family members? It's obvious that the answer is because God so loved the world . . . His love reaches down and renews us so we can love others."

—Chris (parent)

Our Volunteers

Our volunteers are the hands and feet of Jesus. They're actively serving, loving, holding hands, and giving high fives to the guests. And while they're busy serving selflessly, they are the recipients of true fulfillment.

"I'm thankful for being able to be alongside kids and their families, having actual fun, and experiencing joy at its most natural, as well as the opportunity to volunteer and give back so that others may enjoy the many blessings my family was able to experience!"

—Missy K. (volunteer)

"I'm thankful for the opportunity to spend time with an amazing group of kids and adults. They teach me something every time I'm with them."

—Barb (volunteer)

"One of the things I enjoy most about being with the special guests at ZA, and that I have told others about, is the kind way they treat each other. Our guests have such different levels of ability and special needs, yet I've noticed there's no 'hierarchy' or cliques. The way they look out for and help each other warms my heart. Another thing I've often appreciated is the way our guests delight in the simple things of life. They're so happy to open up and share their feelings and experiences with us. Lastly, I appreciate the support the volunteers are given, whether it's in appreciation or material things that are needed to do our part of the job."

—Karen (volunteer)

Spring Creek Church

Spring Creek Church supports the ministry of Zachariah's Acres by sharing their time, talents, and treasure on our campus through volunteer days, service projects, and financial support. Members of Spring Creek Church plan, volunteer, and love families each year at Creation Camp. Creation Camp is a favorite experience for families as they enjoy worship in the tree house, sharing a meal together, and learning about the wonder of God's Creation.

"The Bible teaches that children, all children, matter to God; that Jesus loves children, gave His life on the cross for children, and wants to have a forever relationship with children. God has clearly demonstrated the extent of His investment in those children and their families. Can there be any investment of our time, talent, and treasure more worthy than those children and their families? We are proud to partner with Zachariah's Acres, which provides dignity, value, and opportunity for children with special needs and their families to know the love God and His people have for them."

—Pastor Tom Price (Executive Pastor at Spring Creek Church and board member of ZA)

The Impact of Your Support

At Zachariah's Acres, children with special needs, and their families, are welcomed and accepted as they experience new adventures together. The generous support of churches, family foundations, businesses, and individuals allows us to acknowledge and love more special guests who are yearning for positive affirmation. In light of the importance of our work and the scarcity of any other resources for opportunities, we need your help to serve the next 100,000 special guests by offering more opportunities for children with special needs. Our accessible campus is a declaration of compassion and evidence of your investment.

"I am blessed to be a part of an organization that is inspiring the lives of those with special needs, but what is amazing is how they are an inspiration to all of us."

—Cindy Pagenkopf (board member)

"Though I strive to serve those with special needs, through my involvement with Zachariah's Acres, I'm continually the one who is more blessed. The families that come to ZA are unconditionally welcomed and loved in a way that demonstrates Christ's love in a pure and sincere manner. It's a blessing to play a very small part in this endeavor."

—Jeff Kerlin (Vice President of ZA)

"I serve on the board of ZA to come alongside the amazing journey God has laid out for the children and families we serve; to see the impossible made possible by the many friends and volunteers who share their blessings with others; and to see God's glory shine down on this refuge and those who are blessed through their generosity."

—Alan Petelinsek (board member)

"All deserve to be loved and accepted as the children of God, to be comfortable in their environment, to maximize their skill set, and make their mark on the world. At Zachariah's Acres, this is the standard, not the exception. I am grateful for the opportunity to play the small role I can to make this happen."

—BJ Westfahl (board member)

Community Partners

Our ministry exists to serve children with special needs, yet it requires the support and generosity of the entire community.

There is a place for you at Zachariah's Acres. If you are a person of faith, God's artistry is displayed in countless ways on our campus and through our guests. If you are an educator looking for a place to grow, there's something to learn. If you believe in the strength of the family unit, there's something for you at our family events. If you believe in sustainable agriculture, we treasure and uphold God's Creation. If you've built a business or you're an entrepreneur, there are boundless ways for you and your employees to serve.

"Our program is so honored to partner with Zachariah's Acres. The adults with disabilities in our program enjoy their time volunteering and interacting with nature in this beautiful place. The chickens are some of our best friends and gathering eggs is a favorite activity. The group also enjoys the gardens—to be a part of the process from planning to planting, weeding, and watering, all the way to harvest. It is amazing to learn how plants grow and to see it in action. Zachariah's Acres provides amazing opportunities for our group to experience nature, try new things, and learn new skills."

—Jodi (YMCA)

....

"Zachariah's Acres is a phenomenal facility and also a place with loving and caring staff and volunteers. The team works hard to create a unique place for families with special needs kids to go where they can relax, have fun, and be themselves."

—Jerry Schneider
(Oconomowoc Kiwanis Breakfast Club)

David

David is a young adult with cerebral palsy. He began coming to Zachariah's Acres as part of the Oconomowoc High School Transition program, and once he graduated he wanted to continue volunteering. He loves to plant in the gardens, water the greenhouse, feed the chickens, and wash eggs. According to David, being at ZA is not *"just all work, and no fun! But after getting my work done, I get to hike in the woods, play cards in the tree house, or go snowshoeing."* Because of the supportive and caring staff and volunteers at ZA, David has learned to do things that are usually hard to do, like growing vegetables and fruit.

Meaningful Work for Our Guests

Visit Zachariah's Acres during the week and you will encounter students from several high school transition programs, young adults with special needs, volunteers, and community partners working together.

Participants in Zachariah's Acres Seed to Sale Program or Garden Club learn how to plan, plant, grow, and harvest produce. These two programs highlight the meaningful work of our special guests.

Participants have fun while learning important life skills such as punctuality, positive attitude, follow-through, work ethic, accomplishment, enthusiasm, and teamwork. Fresh fruit and vegetables are used within the classrooms, donated to local food pantries, sold at community farm markets, and used for our Community Supported Agriculture program. At Zachariah's Acres, our guests thrive because they are encouraged to be the authors of their own lives.

Production Greenhouse

The 5,040-square-foot production greenhouse, constructed in the fall of 2020, provides a year-round learning environment for guests of Zachariah's Acres. Educational opportunities abound in this heated year-round space. Guests enjoy learning the importance of healthy eating, environmental stewardship, and social and vocational skill development. It also provides the community and local food pantries with fresh produce. The greenhouses are preferred destinations for our guests, especially on a sunny winter day in Wisconsin.

GOD IS THE BEST ARTIST!

48 Acres of Accessibility

80 CHICKENS AND 14 DUCKS
Americana, Barred Rock,
Rhode Island Reds, ISO Reds

OVER 4,587 FISH CAUGHT
Bass, Bluegill, Perch

9,000+
Evergreen trees

250 DWARF APPLE TREES
Empire, Golden Delicious,
Pink Lady, McIntosh, Gala

4,900+ SQUARE FEET
Raised garden beds

16,500 POUNDS OF PRODUCE GROWN EACH SEASON
Strawberries, lettuce, tomatoes,
squash, zucchini, apples

60 BEEHIVES
Each produces 100 pounds
of honey

10 ACRES
Prairie grass and wildflowers

THE STORY OF ZACHARIAH'S ACRES

Molly

Molly started visiting Zachariah's Acres with the YMCA Service without Boundaries programs in 2016. Molly has a positive, can-do attitude and finds a way to persevere in every circumstance. Over the years, Molly has enjoyed planting in the greenhouses, especially in the winter. Molly snowshoed for the very first time at Zachariah's Acres. Carol, Molly's mom, shared the photo of Molly snowshoeing with family and friends. It was a big "wow" moment for Carol and her family and a good workout for Molly, as she was tired at the end of her trek.

Molly gives back to the ZA community by helping with the Garden Basket CSA (Community Supported Agriculture) programs. During the summer, she distributes produce to community members, always quick to smile and share a story about the plants she tended. Molly's knack to pick out the best tomato in the bunch is a highlight for Garden Basket members.

> "A little dirt never hurt! I love working in the gardens at ZA."
>
> —Molly

Nature-Based Experiences

We host free, year-round, nature-based experiences for children with special needs and their families. When families attend one of our signature events, they create life-long memories, enhance social skills, strengthen family relationships, and simply relax in nature. Favorite activities include fishing, guided nature walks and rolls through prairie grass and wildflowers, snowshoeing, sleigh rides, hay wagon rides, apple picking, or cooking in our educational kitchen.

More than 38 schools, nonprofits, and community partners visit Zachariah's Acres on a regular basis for educational field trips, outdoor recreation, and hands-on learning. For students with special needs, learning new things and participating in nature can be a challenge. We "build to the chair," so if children in wheelchairs can fish, feed chickens, pick berries, visit the tree house, etc., everyone else can as well. We provide customized, nature-based activities for special education departments or small groups of students with special needs. Nature-based experiences for students include hay wagon rides, fishing, snowshoeing, walks/rolls through nature, gardening, berry picking, cooking demonstrations, crafts, and more.

Angelique

"From the first moment at Zachariah's Acres, we were fully accepted and treated like family. Ang is normally wary of new people and gets overwhelmed by new places, but at Zachariah's Acres no one pushed her to be or feel any way other than who she is and how she feels. That kind of acceptance paired with the accessibility of the garden and chicken coop and the full expanse of the farm has sparked such an interest in gardening and how plants and animals grow."

—Charlotte (parent)

GOD IS THE BEST ARTIST!

A Snowy Day at ZA

It was a snowy November morning when the bus pulled up to Zachariah's Acres with eight students from MPS Kluge Elementary. Eighty percent of the students required adaptive equipment (wheelchairs or walkers) for mobility. The students bundled up for their farm tour, including a bumpy hay wagon ride and roll through our accessible orchard and gardens. The snowy weather didn't stop these miraculous students from having fun outside. Upon leaving, one mother came up to our staff and shared, *"Thank you for following through on what you say and having a truly welcoming and accessible place for my child to visit. We made amazing memories today and I actually felt like his mom."* Through tears, she shared how often her son is overlooked or unable to participate in family traditions because of mobility challenges. For that day, they were able to be mother and son instead of caregiver and patient.

Winter

During the winter, our heated barn allows us to offer life-enriching experiences while encouraging families to explore the outdoors. Popular activities are snowshoeing, ice carving demonstrations, dog sled rides, planting in the heated greenhouses, and horse-drawn sleigh rides. Winter experiences include our Christmas Tree Fundraiser, Sleigh Rides for Special Kids, Winterfest, and the Wild Game Lunch Fundraiser.

THE STORY OF ZACHARIAH'S ACRES

Spring

As the weather warms and flowers bloom, guests get to spend more time outdoors. At our DIY workshop, guests learn new skills like building a bird house or making a windowsill herb garden. The annual Mother's Day event allows moms and female caregivers to relax while their kids participate in fun activities. Visitors enjoy planting in our raised gardens, kite-flying, nature walks, helping stock our pond, and naming our baby chicks.

Fundraisers include Community Supported Agriculture (CSA) subscriptions and the Spring Trail Run/Walk/Roll.

GOD IS THE BEST ARTIST!

Summer

Summer is a busy time for guests and volunteers at ZA. It's the height of our Garden Basket CSA (Community Supported Agriculture) season. The community enjoys produce grown, harvested, and packaged by our special guests. Nature-based experiences for our families abound in the warmer months, with fishing, picnics, campfires, and enjoying freshly harvested watermelon with friends on the tree house observation deck. Two signature fundraisers also take place during the summer months—Dinner Under the Stars (our farm-to-table dinner onsite) and the annual Golf Outing and dinner auction.

THE STORY OF ZACHARIAH'S ACRES

Fall

Fall is the season of abundance and gratitude. We celebrate the harvest with hay wagon rides, pumpkin bowling, apple picking, and campfires at our Fall Harvest Fest. Community events and fundraisers include Fall Harvest Dinner (a farm-to-table dining experience) and our Trail Run/Walk/Roll, where participants explore accessible trails through nature.

GOD IS THE BEST ARTIST!

Lessons From Our Community

"Brothers and sisters, think of what you were when you were called. Not many of you were wise by human standards; not many were influential; not many were of noble birth. But God chose the foolish things of the world to shame the wise; God chose the weak things of the world to shame the strong . . . Therefore, as it is written: 'Let the one who boasts boast in the Lord.'"

—1 Corinthians 1:26, 27, and 31

Acceptance

We welcome guests and their families with acceptance and love, by smiling, making eye contact, acknowledging everyone, using first names, and treating them as royalty, because they too are God's children.

A child who might behave in a way that's deemed inappropriate in a public setting can feel welcome at Zachariah's Acres because they won't be looked at strangely. They're not asked to leave if they have a meltdown or do something that might make others feel uncomfortable. It can be a huge relief for families to know acceptance and love without judgement.

Accessibility

We've constructed wheelchair-height nesting boxes, an accessible hay wagon ramp, a paved path in our fruit orchard, and an ADA switch-back ramp to the tree house. It's important that a child in a 300-pound electric wheelchair can explore and immerse themselves in nature along with their friends. We believe that nature should be accessible in order that all may appreciate God's artistry.

Beyond just having fun at Zachariah's Acres, we encourage our guests to slow down and notice God's miraculous Creation. Take a walk/roll, discover tiny Monarch caterpillars, and witness the miracle of those caterpillars morphing into beautiful butterflies.

Faith

"Faith without works is dead." —James 2:26

We are willing to do the work necessary to serve while trusting God to determine the outcome. The investment of sweat equity does not necessarily yield immediate results. Yet faith in God's grace prepares us for the next chapter of servitude. Our faith encourages us to remain others-focused. Faith, hope, and love are consistently and abundantly shared at ZA. As one young lady explained to a new classmate, *"At ZA I work hard, have fun, and see Jesus."*

Courage

Courage is a common theme at Zachariah's Acres. In the winter we go snowshoeing with our special guests, a first for the majority of them. It takes courage to try something new. We stumble often and sometimes fall, but a friend offers a hand to get up and keep going. At the end of the half-mile hike within the pine trees, the smiles of accomplishment are contagious.

The courage to stretch beyond perceived boundaries and create space for adventure and fun reminds each guest, parent, teacher, and care provider that words have the power to destroy or build up those in our lives. Courage can certainly be found in giant leaps of faith, but often we see it in the strength it takes to face another day with joy, purpose, and gratitude. Courage is unleashed through encouragement!

THE STORY OF ZACHARIAH'S ACRES

Purpose

Our trained volunteers lead small groups of young adults to plant and harvest produce, care for the chickens, wash eggs, make flower bouquets for neighboring hospice patients, and prepare crafts and activities for our family events. Many special guests aren't accustomed to physical labor. It's a balance to find the right position for each guest to flourish, but also push them outside of their comfort zone. We've found that providing a positive and supportive environment allows our guests to try new experiences.

One of our guests who is non-verbal typed at the end of his volunteer shift, *"Thank you for giving me meaningful work."* We believe that every person was born with a calling and can make the world a more beautiful place, whether that's through planting and tending to a flower or artfully arranging washed eggs in a carton.

Support

Our primary target population is children and young adults with cognitive and physical disabilities, as well as their families. We encourage families to bring siblings to enrich family relationships and participate in life-long memories. When families witness their son or daughter catch their first fish it supersedes a social media post. Our volunteer team is also trained to lend support to families. While we are not a drop-off facility, our volunteers act as ambassadors for families and single parents to ensure they have the best experience possible.

No Job Too Small

We hold our special guests and volunteers to a high standard because we believe "Whoever can be trusted with very little can also be trusted with much . . ." (Luke 16:10). Our ministry and team are the body of Christ, serving and loving His precious children. The community operates like a body—the head is not more important than the feet or the hands. They all work together to make things happen. Staff, board members, and volunteers at every level perform similar tasks and get their hands dirty. Everyone contributes their skills and learns from helping wherever they see a need with a selfless and positive attitude.

Blessed by Our Guests

Our ministry enriches not only the lives of our special guests, but also imparts change in the lives of our volunteers. A seasoned gardener approached us to help care for our raised gardens. She initially wanted to garden and felt inadequate to work with our special guests. However, we began to have special guests work with her and eventually she requested to have two or three special guests work consistently with her during her shift. She shared with us, "*I signed up to garden but found out I love working with people with special needs.*"

Nature-Based Activities

Several years ago during a planning meeting, a volunteer mentioned that his favorite childhood memory was building a birdhouse in the backyard with his grandfather. That simple idea sparked a concerted effort at Zachariah's Acres to provide simple, nature-based activities for guests. We don't offer activities in nature; we offer nature-based activities.

> "Melissa loves coming to Zachariah's Acres, and we are so grateful to have meaningful work for her to do! She is proud to volunteer and tells everyone about her work in the gardens and greenhouses. We thank the Lord for your ministry."
>
> —Kathy (parent of ZA gardener Melissa)

Flexibility

During the inception of ZA, a nonprofit leader shared this piece of advice: *"Above all else, be flexible."* Flexibility is a constant theme at Zachariah's Acres. We learned early on to be flexible on a day when 200 people came to ZA as the wind had blown our tents out of the ground. We learned to adapt to unpredictable weather by planning multiple indoor and outdoor activities for our guests. We've learned to be flexible when volunteers and groups cancel or bring more people than registered. Flexibility has allowed us to grow and adapt to best serve our guests and families.

Sufficient Grace

Building a ministry that serves children with special needs has its challenges. The days of physical labor, planning, forging partnerships, advocating for our guests, and handling unpredictable Midwestern weather provided numerous openings for God's grace. It's not about the do; it's about the who.

God allows challenges and obstacles so that we may rely on His grace. Without His power at work within us, we would still be serving guests in a farm field, under tents. Each challenge has refined and reaffirmed our calling to serve, love, and be committed to the families and guests of ZA.

The Power of Prayer

We begin every staff meeting and event at Zachariah's Acres with a prayer. It's a time to stop, breathe, gather together, and honor our Chairman of the Board, God. Often a volunteer chaplain, board member, or family will lead us through verses that reflect a theme found in nature, or we take time specifically to pray for our guests. Prayer shifts our eyes to our Creator, unites us in a common vision, and encourages us to continue during difficult seasons.

GOD IS THE BEST ARTIST!

Truths From Our Campus

"But he said to me, 'My grace is sufficient for you, for my power is made perfect in weakness.' Therefore I will boast all the more gladly about my weaknesses, so that Christ's power may rest on me."

—2 Corinthians 12:9

Strength is found when we rely on God's grace.

"Blessed is the one who does not walk in step with the wicked or stand in the way that sinners take or sit in the company of mockers, but whose delight is in the law of the Lord, and who meditates on his law day and night. That person is like a tree planted by streams of water, which yields its fruit in season and whose leaf does not wither—whatever they do prospers."

—Psalm 1:1-3

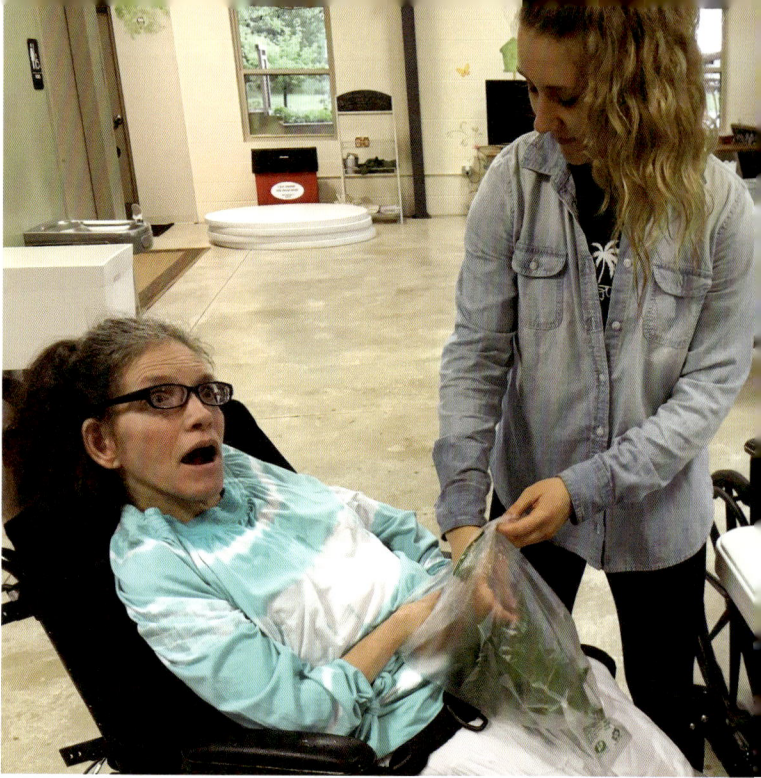

Never underestimate the power of acknowledgment, acceptance, and love.

"Do not forget to show hospitality to strangers, for by so doing some people have shown hospitality to angels without knowing it."

—Hebrews 13:2

Look for the good and be grateful for the impossible or difficult things in your life. God laughs at the word impossible.

"Trust in the LORD with all your heart and lean not on your own understanding."

—Proverbs 3:5

God made you with gifts and skills to impact your family, community, and the world.

"For you created my inmost being; you knit me together in my mother's womb. I praise you because I am fearfully and wonderfully made; your works are wonderful, I know that full well. My frame was not hidden from you when I was made in the secret place, when I was woven together in the depths of the earth. Your eyes saw my unformed body; all the days ordained for me were written in your book before one of them came to be."

—Psalm 139:13-16

There is great power in humility and enthusiasm.

"Jesus said, 'Let the little children come to me, and do not hinder them, for the kingdom of heaven belongs to such as these.'"

—Matthew 19:14

"A little bit better, a little bit different."

"The King will reply, 'Truly I tell you, whatever you did for one of the least of these brothers and sisters of mine, you did for me.'"

—Matthew 25:40

God's Creation heals and restores. When in doubt, go plant in the garden!

Get Involved

"But he was pierced for our transgressions, he was crushed for our iniquities; the punishment that brought us peace was on him, and by his wounds we are healed."

—Isaiah 53:5

Pray

One of the most powerful ways you can get involved in what God is doing at Zachariah's Acres is to join us in prayer. Please pray for the physical, emotional, and spiritual health of our guests; wisdom for our team to serve well; blessings on all those who visit our campus; and courage to be bold in our faith.

- Pray for the health and safety of our special guests and families.
- Pray for the volunteers and staff to serve with authenticity and excellence.
- Pray for blessings upon each person who visits ZA.
- Pray for the wisdom and leadership of our board.
- Pray for blessing and provision on our ministry.

THE STORY OF ZACHARIAH'S ACRES

Families worship together in the tree house at Creation Camp.

Volunteer

Our ministry requires the assistance of many hands to ensure a fun, safe, and memorable experience. We appreciate our volunteers and are fortunate to have many enthusiastic individuals who give of their time. Volunteers bring their personal and professional skills to serve God's special children.

- Ambassadors for our special guests
- Garden and grounds crew
- Chicken volunteers
- Church and business service days
- Eagle Scout or Gold Award projects
- Fundraisers and family nature-based experiences
- Professional skills (crafts, construction, website design, bookkeeping, etc.)

Donate

Fundraising is an ongoing endeavor at Zachariah's Acres. We are seeking community partners, donors, and other supporters to assist us in this important work. The eternal impact is sustainable because of the generosity of the community. Thank you!

- Establish a recurring monthly gift.
- Contribute in-kind services or materials.
- Make a gift of stocks or bonds.
- Sponsor or attend a fundraising event (Wild Game Lunch, Dinner Under the Stars, Golf Outing, Trail Run/Walk/Roll, Christmas Tree Fundraiser, and more).
- Support our Garden Basket CSA program.

We cannot do this without God, but He can certainly do it without us!

Share

Our campus is built to welcome and accommodate children with special needs and their families. If you know someone who would benefit from Zachariah's Acres, please share our website and upcoming family events! Please note that family events are exclusively for children with special needs and their families.

Take Action

Zachariah's Acres is a ministry that highlights all of God's Creation, including *you*! He is the *best* artist! Our heart of service doesn't just exist when our volunteers, staff, or guests are on-site. We carry the values of Zachariah's Acres (faith, authenticity, compassion, excellence, servitude) into our daily lives and throughout the community. We encourage you to take action and join our mission to connect children with special needs, and their families, to the miracles of nature so they may know their Creator.

Begin by acknowledging and interacting with people who have special needs. Who is in your community? The bagger at your grocery store, the local Special Olympics team, the greenhouse employee, or someone else? Everyone can make a difference by treating "the least of these" with respect, love, and kindness.

If you feel called to serve, ask yourself how you can become involved in your community with special children. Connect with your church, YMCA, or schools in your area to see if there are volunteer opportunities to help people with special needs.

If you would like to get involved with our ministry, please contact us for a tour or phone conversation. Whether you know someone we can serve or would like to volunteer, participate in an event, or join our team of prayer warriors, we have a place for you at Zachariah's Acres.

For more information or to get involved with Zachariah's Acres, please visit ZachariahsAcres.org

Connect With Zachariah's Acres

If you would like to learn more about how you can be a part of the ZA community, contact us for a tour. Our campus is open by appointment and during regularly scheduled events. We can't wait to meet you and share what God has done at ZA!

CONTACT US

WEBSITE:
ZachariahsAcres.org

EMAIL:
info@zachariahsacres.org

CAMPUS LOCATION:
N74 W35911 Servants' Way
Oconomowoc, WI 53066

MAILING ADDRESS:
16575 Patricia Ln
Brookfield, WI 53005

THE STORY OF ZACHARIAH'S ACRES

Acknowledgments

God is able to do immeasurably more than we could ask or imagine.
(Ephesians 3:20, common paraphrase)

Thank you to our Creator, Provider, Sustainer, Healer, Shepherd, and Heavenly Father; You are the Chairman of our Board and without Your grace and mercy, we would not exist. A special thank you goes out to the team that helped make *God Is the Best Artist!* happen: Alan and Lisa Petelinsek, the team at Aloha Publishing, Megan Terry, Fusion Creative Works, and the servants and guests of Zachariah's Acres. God had a good day when He made you!

Thank You for Helping Us Grow

ZachariahsAcres.org

May God be glorified in all His designs.